$\mathscr{S}$COTTISH HOME BAKING

SCOTTISH HOME BAKING

Have fun with
some of these recipes
Sue
lots of love
Judy
aug 26th 2011

JUDY PATERSON

SCOTTISH HOME BAKING

First published 1993 by
© Judy Paterson & Lindsay Publications

ISBN 1-898169-00-4

Front cover photograph supplied by **Peter Murray**
Food Stylist **Zoe Kean**
Jacket photograph features "Ye Olde Inn", Davidsons Mains, Edinburgh and
"Edinburgh Marketing Tartan."
Text and cover illustrations by **Gilbert Gordon**

Text layout and cover designed by **Smith & Paul Associates, Glasgow**

Printed and bound by Bell and Bain Ltd., Glasgow

ACKNOWLEDGEMENTS

To all those who have helped, offered advice, donated recipes, tasted and criticized the finished results I owe many thanks. I especially wish to thank Chris Moran, of the James Thin Coffee House, Mrs Baillie and Laura MacDonald of Brora, and Mrs Margaret Paton. Thanks also to my friends in the booktrade for their support and encouragement.

Every effort has been made to ensure those recipes compiled from archival sources are correct. All recipes are given in Imperial and Metric weights and measures.

CONTENTS

INTRODUCTION

I suppose my interest in food and cooking began as a small child during the aftermath of World War Two. I was aware of the scarcity of food and the way in which we "made do". Sweets and cakes were such rare treats I cannot remember them.

After we had moved to Australia the most exciting thing about Friday afternoons was coming home to a house full of the smells of baking – the hot oven, the flour, the rich, spicy smells and above all, ginger. I remember mother inventing "measle" buns when we were all down with that childhood illness. Perhaps I remember most of all, Anzac biscuits, those simple oaty treacly snaps which commemorated the Australian and New Zealand Alliance of World War One!

Food, and especially baking, reflects our culture and heritage in these simple ways.

Years later I began baking through necessity since, where we lived in Papua New Guinea, there were no pastry shops. Unexpected guests were best satisfied with scones or 'pikelets' as I knew them, girdle or drop scones to the Scots. In other words, we made best use of simple ingredients. It was all we had.

When I found myself in the Highlands of Scotland with a hotel to run, once again I had returned to those wonderful floury, warm and fruity smells of childhood. My staff were many and varied, their skills mostly handed down from their mothers and grandmothers. I started a tea room and along with the faded old photographs, donated to decorate the 'Coach House', came the recipes.

After a while it became apparent that scones were best baked by a particular staff member, the best pastry left in the hands of another. Still other staff members ignored the 'hotel' recipes and baked as they had been taught, using recipes which no-one had written down.

Because I was training younger staff for formal qualifications, I was able to collect recipes over a period of time. They are mostly traditional since this was the theme of my tea room which was both a place for the locals of Brora, Sutherland, and a welcome respite for tourists. Of course the tea room was a Scottish invention – that of Miss Cranston of Glasgow in the 1880's.

Other recipes I have added to this collection because they are interesting. Some have been given to me, by friends who are professional; other recipes were passed on to me by my mother-in-law, many of these having belonged to her mother-in-law and that lady's mother before her. It was she who attended cookery classes during the year previous to her marriage. I have wondered if she attended those classes run by D. Williamson and Son, Bakers and Confectioners of Dundas Street, Edinburgh. Had she tried his famous Holyrood Pudding?

Her wonderful handwritten, faded and splattered notebook speaks of women who brought up large families in trying times. Tucked away in the back of this book is an old magazine cutting describing how one might make bedside rugs from twenty pairs of old silk stockings!

The microwaved Cloutie Dumpling is my own, devised to satisfy the constant demand by the men in my life. Most women who have learned to handle their microwave ovens have lent a hand at adapting favourite recipes. I include one passed on to me by Maggie Mackenzie. Doubtless there are a dozen varieties of microwaved Clouties breeding all over Scotland.

And that is the essence of Scottish Baking. Evolving over the centuries it has made use of the produce and implements to hand. A recipe can only give the basic ingredients and methods. Perhaps Love is the unwritten agent of leavening in successful baking; that and the simple pleasure in producing something from one's own hands.

"Joys shared with others are the more enjoyed"

SCONES

W hat could be simpler yet more memorable than the homely scone? It was Queen Victoria's favourite afternoon fare. They are a great favourite today with tourists. In all their varieties, they are a staple feature of morning or afternoon tea for us all.

I n Scotland our strong link with the Low Countries is recalled in our art and architecture, especially round the coast of Fife, when trade during the 16th Century influenced much of our heritage. The scone was probably a development of the Dutch 'Schoonbrot', a fine bread.

T he grains used in these breads, bannocks or 'scones' reflect the agricultural diversity, or poverty, of the country and its various, sometimes harsh regions.

A n open fire was the only method of cooking in most homes until last century. Bread dough was taken to the village bakers for baking – or bought already baked, generally once a week and the simple bannocks and scones were served as every day fare.

$\mathscr{S}$CONE FLOUR

Scone Flour can be made in bulk and stored in airtight containers. The longer it is kept, the lighter will be your scones.

Simply sieve together, 4lb white flour, 2oz cream of tartar and 1oz bicarbonate of soda. (Alternatively these ingredients, in each recipe, may be substituted by Self Raising Flour.)

Using buttermilk, or milk freshly soured with lemon juice with the above traditional recipe will produce scones that are both sharp-tasting and moist. Experiment and remember, almost every Scots housewife has her own favoured recipe. The greatest secret lies in 'light handling' – kneading should only shape the dough.

Scones are wonderful when served warm from the oven, with butter, jam and cream. They will also freeze well and will thaw quickly at room temperature. They may be thawed on the defrost of a microwave and brought to a 'just warm' temperature most successfully!

PLAIN SCONES

8oz(225g) plain flour

1 tspn bicarbonate of soda

1¹/₂ tspns cream of tartar

a pinch of salt

1oz(25g) butter

a little milk

Oven 425F/220C/Gas 7

Sift the dry ingredients into a bowl and rub in the butter, or place sifted dry ingredients into a food processor and using a blade, 'cut' in the butter, so that the mixture is soft and smooth. Add sufficient milk to make a soft but not sticky dough.

Knead the dough lightly on a floured surface and roll or pat into a thickness of $^3/_4$ inch. Use a large scone cutter to make your rounds, re-rolling the scraps and cutting again.

Bake the scones on a lightly greased and floured tray for about 10 minutes. They will rise and should be golden brown.

Place on a wire tray to cool.

SWEET SCONES

8oz(225g) plain flour
¹/₂ tspn bicarbonate of soda
1 tspn cream of tartar
pinch of salt
1 tspn castor sugar
2oz(50g) butter
1 egg (beaten) if liked: milk as
required if no egg used
Oven 425F/220C/Gas Mark 7

Sift dry ingredients as above; rub in butter and add the egg or milk as required to make the soft dough. Some of the egg may be reserved to use for glazing the tops of the scones.

Knead lightly and cut into rounds and bake for 10–15 minutes in a hot oven.

TREACLE SCONES

8oz(225g) plain flour
1 tspn bicarbonate of soda
1 tspn cream of tartar
1 tspn ground ginger
¹/₂ tspn mixed spice
2oz(50g) butter
1 tblespn black treacle
milk
Oven 425F/220C/Gas Mark 7

Sift the dry ingredients. Heat the butter and treacle and add to the dry ingredients. Add just enough milk to make a soft dough.

Handle lightly, either making two ¹/₂ inch circles, scored deeply into quarters and baked for 12–15 minutes; or, cut into scones and bake 7–10 minutes. Cool on a wire rack and serve just warm with butter.

BASIC SCONES

8oz(225g) flour
2 tspn baking powder
$^1/_2$ tspn salt
2oz(50g) butter/
margarine/lard
(1oz(25g) sugar or other ingredient
as listed below)
5floz(150ml) milk
Oven 425F/220C/Gas 7

Sift dry ingredients and rub in butter. Add sugar (or other ingredients – see below). Stir in milk to make soft dough.

Handle lightly and roll into a round $^3/_4$ inch thick. Use a cutter or mark deeply into quarters with a knife. Brush with egg or milk and bake 7–10 minutes for individual scones, or 10–15 minutes for a round.

Oatmeal Scones : substitute 4oz(110g) of fine oatmeal for 4oz(110g) of the flour.

Afternoon Tea Scones: add a beaten egg to the recipe and use little or no milk.

QUICK AND EASY SCONES

1lb(450g) self raising flour
4oz(110g) margarine
1 tspn baking powder
1oz(25g) sugar (optional)
1 egg
$^1/_3$ pint(190ml) milk

In a machine, mix the flour, margarine, baking powder and sugar (if used). Add the egg and milk to make a soft dough. Knead lightly and cut thick scones (12 approximately). Bake for 15–20 minutes at 425F/220C/Gas Mark 7.

VARIATIONS

Cheese Scones: omit sugar and add 4oz(110g) grated mature cheese and a little cayenne and/or mustard powder.

Fruit Scones: use basic recipe and add dried fruits, mixed peel and or glace cherries up to 2oz(50g).

Brown Scones: use half wholemeal and half white flour.

$\mathscr{T}$RADITIONAL POTATO SCONES

8oz(225g) cooked mashed
*   potato*
$^1/_2$oz(10g) butter
2oz(50g) plain flour
$^1/_4$ tspn salt

Add the butter, salt and flour to the mashed potatoes and roll out very thinly. Cut into squares and triangles and fire on a hot girdle or in a heavy frying pan for about 3 minutes each side. Only lightly brush the cooking surface with oil.

Potato Scones are a great breakfast treat alongside bacon and eggs. They are a treat on their own served hot, with a dot of butter.

$\mathscr{S}$ODA SCONES

1lb(450g) plain flour
1 tspn salt
1 tspn bicarbonate of soda
10floz(300ml) buttermilk,
approximately

Sift the dry ingredients and gradually stir in the buttermilk to make a soft dough which should not be sticky.

Turn it on to a floured board and knead only just enough to have a smooth dough. Shape into a round and mark into eight wedges.

Bake for about 30 minutes at 400F/200C/Gas Mark 6, or until it is golden brown.

SOUR SKONS FROM ORKNEY

Soak 8oz(225g) fine oatmeal in 10floz(300ml) buttermilk and leave in a cool place for two or three days.

8oz(225g) plain flour
1 tspn bicarbonate of soda
pinch of salt
1–2 tspns caraway seeds
1oz(25g) caster sugar

Stir the oatmeal mixture and into this add the sifted flour, salt and bicarbonate of soda. Mix well. Add the sugar and caraway seeds.

Mix into a soft dough using more buttermilk if required. Turn onto a floured board. With as little handling as possible, shape the dough into two rounds about $^3/_4$ inch(2cm) thick. Divide each round into four or six wedges and bake on a hot girdle for 10 to 15 minutes on each side.

Wrap the skons in a cloth and cool on a wire rack.

COOKING WITH THE GIRDLE

The Scots Girdle is a heavy platter of cast iron with a looped handle. It can rest on the embers of a fire or on the top of a Range or stove. From ancient times, Culross, in Fife, claimed the monopoly in manufacturing the Girdle – a lucrative trade acknowledged and re-established by James VI in 1599.

An even earlier tradition involves Robert the Bruce who was concerned that his army was adequately fed. The staple he required was the humble oatcake, the 'hard tack' which provided the carbohydrate energy his fighting men needed. Bread might indeed be the staff of life – in Scotland it was the oatcake cooked, of course, on the humble girdle – the ideal portable kitchen.

The girdle should be heated slowly over a low heat so that the cooking temperature will be even. This applies to modern aluminium variations. The girdle should be very lightly oiled and should never be washed. Using buttermilk or freshly soured milk in recipes for the girdle produces better results.

The modern approximation might be the electric frypan or one can use a heavy cast iron frypan.

DROP SCONES/SCOTCH PANCAKES

Heat the girdle or frypan slowly.
8oz(225g) plain flour
1 tspn cream of tartar
1 tspn bicarbonate of soda
1oz(25g) caster sugar
pinch of salt
1 egg slightly beaten
5floz(150ml) milk

Sift the dry ingredients and add the egg and a little milk to a well in the centre. Blend the mixture evenly and gradually add the rest of the milk to form a batter.

Test the temperature of the girdle or pan by dropping a teaspoonful of the batter onto the cooking surface. You should see air bubbles on the surface within a few seconds. Turn the pancake which will be brown, in order to cook the other side. Gauge the time in order to prevent burning.

Cook the rest of the batter in batches – use a dessert spoon to form 'two bite' pancakes. You may need to add a little more grease in between batches. Keep the pancakes warm in a tea-towel as you continue cooking.

These are great with butter, jam, cream, honey or anything else you fancy. My first introduction to these was in Australia where they are called Pikelets.

PIKELETS

8oz(225g) Self Raising flour
pinch of salt
$\frac{1}{4}$ tspn bicarbonate of soda
1 egg beaten
5floz(150ml) milk at room
temperature to which is added
1 tspn vinegar
margarine for cooking

Mix dry ingredients thoroughly. Whip the egg and milk together and combine with dry ingredients to make a batter. Leave to stand while preparing for fast cooking.

Melt margarine over cooking surface and any surplus can be folded into the batter. Drop spoonfuls onto the cooking surface and proceed as above.

GIRDLE SCONES

8oz(225g) self raising flour
pinch of salt
2oz(50g) butter
scant 5floz(140ml) milk

Mix flour and salt and rub in butter. Make into a soft dough with the milk and knead lightly on a floured surface to make a 1/2 inch(1cm) thick round. Score deeply to make wedges and place on a preheated floured girdle.

Cook for 7–8 minutes and turn to cook the other side. It will be cooked when firm. Test by cutting one of the wedges. It will be trial and error before you have the correct times for your personal cooking implements.

$\mathcal{S}$COTS CRUMPETS

These are thin, almost pancake-like, tea-time fare. They can be spread with jam or honey and are traditionally rolled up for serving.

8oz(225g) plain flour
2 tblspns castor sugar
pinch of salt
2 large eggs, separated
2 tblspns melted butter
15floz(425ml) milk

Beat the egg yolks and blend in the dry ingredients. Add the melted butter and milk to make a batter which is fairly thin. Beat egg whites to soft peaks and add to batter folding with a knife or metal spoon.

Pour large spoonfuls of the batter onto a lightly greased girdle or frypan. The pancake should be about the size of a small breadplate, 4"–5"(13cm) in diameter. The batter should be spread thinly and when golden brown underneath and slightly bubbly on top, turn carefully to cook the other side. Keep them warm by stacking in a clean tea towel.

They should be eaten immediately.

ATCAKES

These are not easy to make, yet were a staple food in many a Scottish household. Nowadays they are commercially produced most successfully, but you may be interested to try your hand at the following recipe.

8oz(225g) medium oatmeal
a generous pinch of salt
1 tblspn dripping or lard
$^1/_4$ tspn bicarbonate of soda
up to 6 tblspns of hot water

Work quickly and have plenty of meal for both your hands and the surface upon which you are working.

Mix the dry ingredients and melt the dripping which is poured into the centre of the mixture. Stir well adding enough of the hot water to make a stiff dough. Traditional recipes suggest the use of a porridge spurtle for this task; use the handle of a wooden spoon as an alternative.

Knead the dough on a surface generously covered with meal and divide the quantity in two. Using plenty of meal roll out two circles to about 1/4 inch(5mm) thick. Cut into wedges and sprinkle with more meal.

Cook these on a medium heated girdle or frypan for about

three minutes (or when the edges begin to curl/brown) or alternatively, for 30 minutes in an oven at 325F/160C/Gas 3.

Oatcakes are served at breakfast with honey and marmalade or at lunches with soup and cheese. They are an ideal accompaniment for main dishes such as salmon or game foods.

EASY OATCAKES

The following recipe uses flour which is not traditional but makes the mixture easier to handle.

8oz(225g) oatmeal
4oz(110g) plain flour
1 tspn baking soda
1 tspn salt
3oz(75g) margarine
milk for mixing

Mix dry ingredients and combine with just melted cooled margarine. You may add a little milk to complete the binding but the mixture should be very stiff. Roll out and shape or cut. Bake in a slow oven, 250F/120C/Gas Mark $^1/_2$ for 45 minutes, or until the edges begin to brown.

$\mathscr{S}$AUTY BANNOCKS

6oz(175g) oatmeal
$^1/_2$ tspn salt
$^1/_2$ tspn bicarbonate of soda
1 tspn sugar
a full tspn syrup
10floz(275ml) milk
1 egg, beaten

Mix the dry ingredients. Stir the syrup into the milk and blend into dry ingredients. Leave the mixture to prove overnight. Add the egg. The batter should not be too thick so you may need extra milk.

Pour a little onto a hot girdle or frypan, tilting the cooking dish to make thin even rounds. Cook on both sides and stack in a teatowel on a wire rack.

$\mathscr{F}$IFE BANNOCKS

6oz(175g) plain flour
4oz(110g) oatmeal
$^1/_2$ tspn bicarbonate of soda
$^3/_4$ tspn cream of tartar
a pinch each of salt and sugar
1 tblspn butter
freshly soured milk or buttermilk

Sift the dry ingredients and rub in the butter. Make into a dough using sufficient milk. Turn on to a floured board and knead lightly. Roll into a round, cut into four and cook on a hot girdle or bake in a hot oven.

*B*ARLEY BANNOCK

8oz(225g) barley flour
2oz(50g) plain flour
¹/₂ tspn salt
1 tspn cream of tartar
1 tspn bicarbonate of soda
10floz(275ml) buttermilk (or
freshly soured milk)

Add the soda to the milk. Sift the dry ingredients. Now add the buttermilk and make into a light, soft dough with little handling. Make a round of about ¹/₂ inch(1cm) thick and cut into wedges. Bake on a medium to hot girdle on both sides, until brown. Keep soft and warm by wrapping in a cloth.

Barley Bannocks originate from the Island of Stornoway.

*B*ARLEY BANNOCKS – BAKED

8oz(225g) plain flour)
8oz(225g) barley flour
generous tspn salt
rounded tspn cream of tartar
1 tspn baking soda: milk

Mix all the dry ingredients and add enough milk to make a fairly soft dough. Turn onto a floured board and knead lightly forming a round bannock about 2 inches(5cm) deep. Prick the top with a fork and bake in a moderate oven, in a tin, for about an hour.

FATTY CUTTIES

6oz(175g) plain flour
3oz(75g) sugar
3oz(75g) currants
3oz(75g) butter or margarine,
melted
pinch of bicarbonate of soda

Sift the flour and bicarbonate of soda and mix in the currants and sugar. Add the melted butter to make a stiff dough. Knead lightly until smooth and divide into two. Roll each portion to a round of about $\frac{1}{4}$"($\frac{1}{2}$cm) thick and cut each into 4–6 wedges. Cook on a hot girdle until brown.

This recipe comes from Orkney and is best eaten on the same
day as cooking.

HORTBREADS AND CAKES

Shortbreads

As with many rich foods, shortbreads were traditionally baked
for Hogmanay and varied regionally. They may be baked in a tin, shaped
into rounds and cut into wedges or even cut into biscuits or fingers.
For a really festive touch use a carved wooden mould.

Shortbreads were probably among the cakes given out on
"Cake Day", the last day of the year, In Fife and other districts, it was the
custom for children to visit their neighbours to "beg" for their cakes.
Several rhymes are recorded but I like this pithy couplet:

> "Our feet are cauld, our shoes are thin,
> Gies our cakes, an' let us rin!"

It is easy to imagine a group of grinning faces as they
ran off with a chunky sugary finger of
buttery shortbread.

ASIC SHORTBREAD

6oz(175g) plain flour
2oz(50g) rice flour
2oz(50g) caster sugar
4oz(110g) butter

Sift together the two flours. Cream the butter and sugar and then work in the flours. Knead until the mixture is smooth and without cracks. Roll into a ball and cut into halves. Roll each to a round of about $\frac{1}{4}$ inch (5mm) in thickness. Pinch the edges and prick the surface with a fork. Bake in a moderate oven, 350F/180C/Mark 4 Gas, for about $\frac{1}{2}$ an hour. Let it cool on the tray and then transfer carefully to a wire rack. Sprinkle with caster sugar and cool completely. *Store in an airtight container.*

ISCUITS AND FINGERS

Use the above recipe but shape into oblong 'fingers' or cut into biscuits, (a scone cutter works well) and prick the tops with a fork. Bake on a tray in a moderate oven for 15–20 minutes and transfer to a wire rack to cook. Sprinkle with caster sugar.

$\mathscr{S}$IMPLE SHORTBREAD

12oz(350g) plain flour
4oz(110g) cornflour
4oz(110g) caster sugar
8oz(225g) butter

$\mathbf{S}$ift the flours together. Cream the butter and sugar thoroughly and then work in the flours. Knead until smooth and without cracks and shape into a round onto a baking sheet. Pinch the edges and prick with a fork. Alternatively, press the mixture into a flat tin, or mould, and prick with fork. Bake in a slow oven, 325F/160C/Mark 3 Gas for about 45 minutes. Cut into wedges or fingers, and sprinkle with caster sugar.

$\mathscr{Q}$UICK AND EASY SHORTBREAD

12oz(350g) plain flour
8oz(225g) margarine
4oz(110g) caster sugar

$\mathbf{M}$ix together in a machine using the pastry blades. Roll out to about $\frac{1}{4}$ inch(5mm) thick and cut large round biscuits with pastry cutters. Bake 30–40 minutes at 325F/160C/Gas Mark 3.

VARIATIONS: Add cherries, nuts, chocolate chips, ginger, fruit or almonds.

PETTICOAT TAILS

8oz(225g) plain flour
4oz(110g) butter
2oz(50g) caster sugar
2 tspns caraway seeds (optional)

Sieve the flour and sugar and rub in the butter. Add the caraway seeds. Knead until smooth and divide into two. Roll each into a round of about $\frac{1}{6}$ inch(4mm) thick (considerably thinner than for other shortbreads). Pinch the edges into scallops and prick with a fork to make a pattern. Cut a circle in the centre and divide the petticoat into wedges. Bake on a greased tray at 350F/ 180C/Mark 4 Gas for 20 to 30 minutes to a pale golden colour. Sprinkle well with caster sugar and allow to cool on the tray.

This delicate shortbread was a speciality of Edinburgh taking its shape from the fashionable hooped petticoats of the nineteenth century, though another explanation suggests the name is a corruption of the French, Petites Gatelles.

AYRSHIRE SHORTBREAD

7oz(200g) plain flour
1oz(25g) rice flour
4oz(110g) caster sugar
4oz(110g) butter
2 tblspns cream mixed with an
egg yolk

Sift the dry ingredients and rub in the butter. Add the cream and egg mix and work into the mixture with a flat knife binding the ingredients. Knead the dough lightly and roll to about $\frac{1}{4}$ inch(5mm) thick. Cut small round biscuits and bake on a greased tray, 350F/180C/Gas Mark 4 for about 15 minutes.

Perhaps it is not surprising that this recipe, from a rich dairy farming district, uses cream.

PITCAITHLY BANNOCK

6oz(175g) plain flour
2oz(50g) cornflour
4oz(110g) caster sugar
8oz(225g) butter
2oz(50g) flanked almonds
2oz(50g) cut peel

Sift the flours. Beat the sugar and butter until light and creamy and mix in the flours. Add most of the almonds and the peel and knead lightly. Form a thick round about 8 inches(20cm) in diameter, mark into wedges with a knife and pinch the edges. Press the rest of the almonds onto the top and transfer the round to a greased baking sheet. Bake at 325F/160C/Gas Mark 3 for $\frac{3}{4}$ to one hour.

 ANTALLON CAKES

This is really a shortbread variation, the name recalling the Borders Castle of Tantallon.

> *4oz(100g) plain flour*
> *4oz(100g) rice flour*
> *pinch of bicarbonate of soda*
> *4oz(100g) butter*
> *4oz(100g) caster sugar*
> *tspn of finely grated lemon rind*
> *2 eggs, beaten*

Sift the flours and bicarbonate of soda. Cream the butter and sugar. Add a little of the egg and a spoonful of flour, creaming thoroughly before adding more egg and flour. Continue until all the flour and the eggs have been mixed in. Add the lemon rind. The dough should be fairly stiff.

* Roll out thinly and cut rounds using a scalloped cutter.
* Bake for about 30 minutes at 350F/180C/Gas Mark 4.
* Sprinkle with caster sugar as they leave the oven.

ONTROSE CAKES

These are lovely afternoon tea-cakes. The quantity makes about 2 dozen.

4oz(100g) self-raising flour
4oz(100g) caster sugar
4oz(100g) butter
3oz(75g) currants, optional
1 tblspn brandy
2 tspns rose-water
a good pinch of ground nutmeg
2 eggs, beaten

Cream the butter and sugar until light and fluffy. Gradually add the beaten eggs and mix well. Add the currants if used and the brandy, rose-water and nutmeg. Mix well. Stir in the flour and combine thoroughly.

Half-fill greased patty-tins or paper cases.
Bake at 375F/190C/Gas Mark 5 for 10 to 15 minutes.

$\mathcal{S}$EED CAKE

6oz(175g) self-raising flour
1 tspn baking powder
1 tspn caraway seeds
4oz(100g) butter
4oz(100g) caster sugar
pinch of nutmeg
2oz(50g) mixed chopped peel
1 tspn brandy
2 drops of rose-water
2 eggs, beaten

Sift the flour and baking powder. Add the dry ingredients and mix well. Cream the butter and sugar and gradually add the beaten eggs. Stir in the brandy and rose-water. Stir in the flour and mix thoroughly.

Grease an eight-inch (20cm) cake tin, line the base and pour in the cake mix. Bake at 350F/180C/Gas Mark 4, for about 45 minutes.

 # IET LOAF

This is a very light sponge, mentioned by Sir Walter Scott in his novel St Ronan's Well. It is an early example of eggs being used as a raising agent.

1lb(450g) caster sugar
8oz(225g) soft butter
6 size 3 eggs, whisked thoroughly
12oz(350g) sifted plain flour
$^1/_2$ tspn ground cinnamon
finely grated peel of a lemon

Cream the butter and sugar until it is light and frothy and gradually beat in the whisked eggs. Beat well for a few minutes.

Add the lemon rind and cinnamon. Gradually add the flour, beating continually to keep the mixture light.

Pour the mixture into a large cake tin which has been lined with well greased paper. Bake for about 35 minutes at 375F/190C/Gas Mark 5.

The cake should be golden brown and well risen. Allow it to cool in the tin, on a rack for about 10 minutes. Remove it from the tin and cool on the wire rack.

The cake may be finished by either sprinkling icing sugar on the top about five minutes before it is cooked or it may be iced when cold.

ONEY CAKES

1lb(450g) plain flour
4oz(100g) butter
2oz(50g) caster sugar
1¹/₂ tspns baking powder
pinch of salt
2 tblspns honey
2 egg yolks

1 egg white
10floz(300ml) milk
topping :
8oz(225g) thick heather honey
mixed with 2 tblspns of ground
almonds.

Rub the butter into the flour. Over a low heat, dissolve the sugar into the honey and add the baking powder. Whisk the egg yolks and blend them with the milk.

To the flour mixture add a little of the honey mix alternately with the egg mixture and combine thoroughly, continuing until the ingredients are mixed well, adding the salt finally.

Roll the paste lightly, on a floured board and cut into rounds or shapes. Bake for about 20 minutes at 350F/180C/Gas Mark 4.

Put the cakes on to a wire rack, brush with egg white and spoon over a little of the topping mix. Set in a cool oven for just a few minutes.

INGERBREADS

The "gingerbreads" we know today are very different from
the early hard biscuits from medieval days when spices were rare and
expensive. Some of the heavy recipes are still favoured but the use of
raising agents allowed the development of the lighter
varieties mostly baked today.

Sir Walter Scott celebrated a great baker of Gingerbreads,
one Mrs Flockart, in his novel Waverley. She was popularly known as
Luckie Fykie and was admired by the great and genteel of Edinburgh as well
as being a great favourite among the young Scott's school chums. Her
gingerbreads included thick, soft cakes as well as Parliament
biscuits and ginger snaps.

As with all Scottish baking, there are traditional
and regional varieties.

EDINBURGH GINGERBREAD

8oz(225g) plain flour

1 tspn bicarbonate of soda

2 tspns ground ginger

1 tspn cinnamon

pinch of salt

6oz(175g) butter

6oz(175g) treacle

4oz(110g) soft brown sugar

6 tblspns milk

2 eggs

2oz(50g) sultanas

2oz(50g) flaked almonds

Sift the flour, spices, salt and soda and stir in the fruit and nuts. Melt the butter with the treacle and sugar on a low heat. The mixture should remain coolish but the sugar dissolved. Add the milk and stir in the eggs. Pour the warm mixture into a well in the centre of the dry ingredients and mix thoroughly to form a batter. Pour into a greased and lined 2lb(1kg) loaf tin.

Bake at 325F/160C/Gas Mark 3 for $1^1/_4$ hours.

This is a fairly heavy recipe and may sink on cooling.

DUNDEE GINGERBREAD

12oz(350g) plain flour
1 tspn ground ginger
1 tspn ground cinnamon
1 tspn baking soda
2oz(50g) butter
3 tblspns golden syrup
4 tblspns treacle
1 egg, beaten
5oz(150ml) milk
6oz(175g) mixed fruit

Sift flour, spices and soda into a bowl. Gently dissolve the milk, syrups and butter and pour into a well in the centre of the dry ingredients. Add the beaten egg and vigorously mix the batter until it is very smooth. Stir in the fruit. Put the mixture into a greased and lined tin and bake at 350F/180C/Gas Mark 4 for about 2 hours.

FOCHABERS GINGERBREAD

8oz(225g) plain flour
4oz(110g) butter or margarine
2oz(50g) caster sugar
1 tspn mixed spice
2 tspns ground ginger
¹/₂ tspn ground cloves
1 tspn ground cinnamon
1 tspn bicarbonate of soda

4floz(110ml) black treacle
1 egg
5floz(150ml) beer
6oz(175g) mixed fruit (with peel)
2oz(50g) ground almonds (optional)

Sift the flour and spices and fold in the dried fruits and ground almonds if used. Cream the butter and sugar until light and fluffy. Melt the treacle and add to the butter mixture, beating in the egg as well. Fold into this mixture the blended dry ingredients. Dissolve the soda in the beer and stir this into the mixture.

Put the mixture into a 7¹/₂ inch(19cm) greased and lined cake tin (or a 1lb(450g) loaf tin) and depress the centre of the mixture which will cook more slowly than the outer edges. Bake in a slow oven, 300F/150C/Gas Mark 2 for about 1¹/₂ hours.

Cool in the tin for a while before turning on to a wire rack.

*G*INGERBREAD SQUARES

1lb(450g) plain flour
8oz(225g) soft brown sugar
6oz(175g) butter or margarine
4 tblspns treacle
$^1/_2$ tspn nutmeg
2 tspns ground ginger
1 tspn ground cinnamon
pinch of salt
2oz(50g) mixed chopped peel
6oz(160ml) buttermilk
2 beaten eggs

Mix all the dry ingredients except the peel. Rub in the butter and add the peel. Melt the treacle to just warm and add the beaten eggs. Add this to the flour mixture and combine thoroughly. Add the buttermilk and beat well. Bake in greased shallow tins in a moderate oven for 30–40 minutes. Cool slightly and cut into squares.

A variation on this is the recipe for Orkney Broonies included in the chapter on Regional specialities.

GINGERBREAD LOAF

In a pan gently warm together:

¹/₂ pint(275ml) milk
2oz(50g) margarine
1 tblspn black treacle
8oz(225g) mixed fruit, and
8oz(225g) granulated sugar.

When the margarine has melted place the warm ingredients into a mixer bowl and add:

> *10oz(275g) self raising flour*
> *1 tspn bicarbonate of soda*
> *¹/₂ tspn mixed spice*
> *1¹/₂ tspn ground ginger, and*
> *1 tspn baking powder.*

Mix thoroughly and place in a greased 2lb(1kg) loaf tin. Bake slowly for 45–60 minutes 325F/160C/Gas Mark 3.

GINGERBREAD MEN

6oz(175g) flour
¹/₂ tspn bicarbonate of soda
1¹/₂oz(35g) lard, or, 2oz(50g) margarine
4oz(110g) golden syrup
1 tspn ground ginger
currants for decoration

Melt the syrup and fat. Sift the flour, bicarbonate of soda and ground ginger and add the melted mixture to make a stiff paste. Roll out thinly and cut shapes with cutter. Place the men on a greased baking sheet and decorate with currants. Bake for 15 minutes, or until golden brown, 350F/180C/Gas Mark 4.

GRANNY'S GINGERBREAD

1lb(450g) plain flour
6oz(175g) margarine
4oz(125g) soft brown sugar
2 tspns ground ginger
2 tspns mixed spice
1 tspn baking soda
1 egg
5floz(150ml) milk
1lb(450g) treacle
a handful of raisins, currants and
chopped crystalized ginger.

Melt the treacle, margarine, sugar and milk over a low heat. Mix the dry ingredients and pour in the melted ingredients with the beaten egg. Mix thoroughly. Bake in a moderate oven for about an hour or more.

Keep the cake for a week before serving.

These were scant instructions for what is a truly delicious totally sticky gingerbread. A large loaf will generally sink in the centre as it cools. I like to make this up into three smaller tins and I line the bottom of the tins. Even better, bake them in the "disposable" metal trays which you can buy, or save from your Chinese Carry-outs!

$\mathcal{G}$INGER SNAPS

8oz(225g) self raising flour
2oz(50g) sugar
1oz(25g) golden syrup
1oz(25g) treacle
1 tspn baking soda
1 tspn ground ginger
3oz(75g) margarine
lemon essence

Melt the syrup, treacle, margarine, sugar and a few drops of lemon essence. Sift the flour, baking soda and ginger. Add the melted liquid and mix thoroughly. Break off small amounts, about the size of a walnut, and roll into balls. Place these, well spaced apart, on a greased baking sheet, and bake for about 15 minutes at 350F/180C/Gas Mark 4.

EDINBURGH TART OR QUEEN MARY'S TART

The following recipe was introduced to me by the latter name with the story that it had been devised as a treat when Mary Queen of Scots first came to Edinburgh. It was certainly a tea time treat and because it is so easy to make, well worth a try.

Line a greased 8"–9"(20–23cm) shallow dish, plate or flan ring with puff pastry and into the centre pour the following mixture;
2oz(50g) sugar dissolved in 2oz(50g) melted butter
to which is added 2oz(50g) chopped candied peel,
1oz(25g) sultanas and 2 beaten eggs.
Bake in a hot oven, 450F/230C/Gas Mark 8 for 15–20 minutes. Use a lower shelf. Or reduce the temperature slightly and bake for 20–30 minutes.

It looks extraordinary but is delicious served either hot or cold with cream.

PARLIES OR SCOTTISH PARLIAMENT CAKES

These are really biscuits, originating in Edinburgh and favoured by the distinguished clientele of one Luckie Fykie who had a shop in Waverley.

8oz(225g) plain flour
4oz(110g) butter or
margarine
2oz(50g) sugar
1 egg
2 tblspns treacle
ground ginger (optional)

Cream the butter and sugar. Add the flour, egg and treacle and mix thoroughly. Use a teaspoon to drop the mixture on to a greased baking sheet and bake at 350F/180C/Gas Mark 4, for 15–20 minutes.

ECCLEFECHAN TARTS

This variation of the border tart is traditionally made into small individual tarts, though it can be made into a larger tart.

Make a shortcrust pastry, as for the Border Tart and cut 12 circles to line a patty tin, or line an 8 inch(20cm) flan ring.

The Filling:
2oz(50g) butter
3oz(75g) soft brown sugar
2 tspns wine vinegar
4oz(110g) mixed dried fruit
1oz(25g) chopped walnuts
1 egg

Melt the butter and stir in the sugar and egg. Add the vinegar, fruit and nuts and spoon into pastry cases.

Bake for 20–25 minutes at 375F/ 190C/Gas Mark 3. Serve hot or cold.

You may note this recipe is not too dissimilar from Queen Mary's tart!

ORDER TART

The original recipe for this rich tart called for a yeasty pastry into which was folded butter. As with the Selkirk Bannock the dough for this would have been a portion from the weekly bread making. Nowadays a rich shortcrust pastry is used.

The Pastry: *6oz(175g) flour)*
3oz(75g) butter or margarine
1oz(25g) caster sugar
1 egg yolk

Rub the butter into the flour, stir in the sugar and bind the mixture to make a firm dough. Line an 8 inch(20cm) flan ring and reserve the extra dough for decoration.

The Custard:*1 tblspn cornflour*
$^1/_2$oz(15g) butter
5floz(150ml) milk
1 egg yolk
1oz(25g) caster sugar
2 drops vanilla essence

Blend the cornflour with a little milk and stir in the remaining milk and sugar. Heat gently until it boils and simmer for a couple of moments before removing from the heat. Stir in the butter and let the custard cool a little before stirring in the egg yolk and vanilla essence. Leave to cool.

The Filling: *4oz(100g) marzipan*
1oz(25g) flaked almonds
1oz(25g) chopped mixed peel

Roll the marzipan to fit the base of the pastry. Sprinkle over the almonds and peel. Spread the cooled custard over this. Using the left over rolled pastry, cut circles of about 1 inch(3cm) in diameter and arrange these in a pattern on top of the custard.

Cover with a circle of greaseproof paper to prevent burning the custard and bake for 20 minutes at 400F/200C/Gas Mark 6 and then for a further 20 minutes in a slower oven, 350F/180C/Gas Mark 4.

Decorate by combining 1oz(25g) icing sugar with a little warm water and spreading over the pastry circles. Serve either hot or cold.

This is a very rich tart and I find the iced pastry circles detract from the otherwise subtle splendour of this treat. Even a latticed decoration seems to heavy for modern tastes. Try a very light shake of nutmeg or cinnamon or decorate with a few flaked almonds instead.

 BERDEEN CRULLA

It is generally thought these plaited doughnuts were introduced to both Scotland and America by the Dutch. A simple variation of this may be found in modern bakery shops where the dough is a twist rather than the traditional plait.

> *2oz(50g) butter at room temperature*
> *2oz(50g) sugar*
> *7oz(200g) self-raising flour*
> *1 egg*
> *oil for deep frying*

Beat the butter and sugar until light and creamy. Beat in the egg. Stir in the flour to make a stiffish dough. Knead until smooth and divide into 6 portions.

Roll each portion to an oblong about 5"–6" long(120cm–150cm). Cut each portion into three strips almost to the end. Plait the strips and seal the end with a little water.

Deep fry until they are quite golden. Drain excess fat and lay them on kitchen paper. Dust with caster sugar or icing sugar and eat either hot or cold.

# BUTTERY ROWIES

The Auld Alliance with France might have been the influence behind this breakfast treat from Aberdeen. It is very similar to a croissant.

> *1lb(450g) strong white flour*
> *1oz(25g) fresh yeast*
> *1 tspn caster sugar*
> *1 tspn salt*
> *6oz(175g) butter at room temperature*
> *6oz(175g) lard*
> *$^1/_2$ pint (300ml) lukewarm water*
> *Oven: 425F/220C/Gas Mark 7*

Stir the sugar into about half of the warm water and add the yeast. Stir and leave in a warm place for 10–15 minutes until it is frothy.

Sift the flour and salt into a bowl and gradually add the yeast mixture, using the extra liquid to make a firm dough. Knead for about 10 minutes and place the dough into a floured bowl. Cover with a clean damp cloth and leave in a warm place to double in size.

Knock back the dough and knead for a few minutes before rolling out into a large rectangle about $^1/_2$ inch(1cm) thick.

Combine the butter and lard and spread one third of the mixture over the top two thirds of the dough. Fold up the bottom third of the dough and fold down over this the top third of the dough. Press the edges to seal and re-roll the dough to near its original size. Leave it to rest for about 10 minutes.

Repeat the process twice more. After the last rolling, cut the dough into 16 squares.

Form the squares into roughly oval shapes by folding in the edges and leave on a greased baking sheet, well spaced, to prove for about 30 minutes in a warm place.

Brush the tops with milk and bake for 15–20 minutes until brown.

They are best eaten warm from the oven with butter.

RKNEY BROONIES

This easy recipe is very similar to the Parkin of Northern England and is really a type of gingerbread.

8oz(225g) fine oatmeal

4oz(100g) self-raising flour

5oz(150g) golden syrup

2oz(50g) black treacle

4oz(100g) soft brown sugar

2 tspns ground ginger

4oz(100g) butter or margarine

$^1/_2$ tspn bicarbonate of soda

5floz(125ml) buttermilk

1 egg

pinch of salt

Oven: 350F/180C/Gas Mark 4

Mix the meal and flour and rub in the butter. Add the other dry ingredients and combine thoroughly. Mix together the syrup, treacle, egg and buttermilk and stir into the dry ingredients. Pour into a greased and lined tin, 8"(20cm) square, and bake for about 35 minutes.

When cool, cut into squares and store in a tin for a week before eating.

ESTIVE FARE

For festive occasions humble bannocks and breads were
enriched with expensive spices and dried fruits. As time passed and
such ingredients became more freely available the Scottish
tradition in tea breads and tea cakes developed.

Bakers today offer a range of tea breads or fruit loaves,
some of these specialities. Favourites from my local baker include a
crusty malty "Youma" fruit loaf and the Knotty loaf, so called
since the light fruity dough is twisted into a knot.

The recipe following is for the most famous
of these 'tea-breads'. It has exceptional keeping
qualities and it is very rich.

SELKIRK BANNOCK

2lb(900g) plain strong flour
4oz(110g) lard
4oz(110g) butter
³/₄ pint (425ml) milk
8oz(225g) sugar
1oz(25g) yeast
1lb(450g) mixed dried fruit (or 8oz(225g)
each currants and sultanas)
pinch salt
milk and sugar for the glaze
Oven preheated to 425F/220C/Gas Mark 7

Sift the flour and salt and add the sugar. Melt the butter and lard and add the milk heating only to blood temperature. Stir in the yeast. Pour the liquid into a well in the centre of the dry mixture and form into a soft dough. Knead on a floured board for about five minutes or more.

Place the dough in a clean warm bowl and cover with a damp cloth. Leave in a warm place until the dough has doubled in size. Turn the dough on to a

$\mathcal{S}$ELKIRK BANNOCK *cont*.

floured board and work in the dried fruits. This quantity will make two large or four small bannocks or rounds which should be bowl shaped. Place them on a greased baking tray and leave them in a warm place to rise again, about 20 minutes.Bake in a hot oven for 15 minutes and then reduce the heat to 375F/190C/Gas Mark 5, and bake for a further 15–20 minutes. Large bannocks will take a little longer.

Prepare the glaze by dissolving 1 tblspn sugar in warm milk. Liberally brush the glaze over the almost cooked bannocks and return them to the oven for the final 15 minutes.

Cool on a wire rack.

These rich moist buns will keep well for several weeks in airtight containers. Serve sliced thinly, spread with butter.

SCOTCH BLACK BUN

Don't be put off by the formidable list of ingredients. The recipe is not as complicated as it looks. The result is a stunning feature for your next Hogmanay.

Pastry: *12oz(350g) plain flour*
3oz(75g) lard
3oz(75g) butter or margarine
pinch salt
cold water

Filling: *1lb(450g) seedless raisins* — *$^1/_2$ tspn ground ginger*
1lb(450g) cleaned currants — *$^1/_2$ tspn ground cinnamon*
2oz(50g) blanched chopped almonds — *$^1/_2$ tspn baking powder*
2oz(50g) chopped mixed peel — *generous pinch of black pepper*
6oz(175g) plain flour — *a large egg beaten*
3oz(75g) soft brown sugar — *tblspn brandy*
1 tspn allspice — *milk*

To make the Pastry:

Grease an 8 inch (20mm) loaf tin. Make the pastry by rubbing the fats into the flour and salt and use enough cold water to make a stiff dough. Roll out $^3/_4$ of the pastry to line the tin and reserve the rest to make a lid.

To make the Filling:

Sift all the dry ingredients together and mix all the fruits thoroughly and then combine the two, adding the brandy. Stir in almost all the beaten egg (reserving a little to glaze the pastry). Add just enough milk to moisten the mixture.

Pack the filling into the pastry-lined tin and cover with the pastry lid. Seal the edges well, lightly prick the lid with a fork. Using a skewer pierce the lid and the mixture 4 or 6 times to allow the steam to escape during baking. Brush the top with the left over beaten egg.

Cook for three hours in an oven, 325F/160C/Gas Mark 3. Cool in the tin, remove, and store in an airtight container.

Black Bun should be made at least one month in advance of Hogmanay since it improves with keeping. It will keep up to six months quite well.

HINT.

I find it easier to cut the pastry into the five pieces which will make up the shell, using the tin as a rough guide for cutting. I then press the very slight overlaps to seal the pastry shell. The slightly thicker "seams" make it easier to get out of the tin.

 UNDEE CAKE

There are no spices in this world famous cake which makes it unusual among the 'festive' recipes. It is however, rich, moist and buttery. It makes an ideal second Christmas cake to have alongside the traditional dark and spicy cake. It is so good, I am sure you will bake it more than just once a year!

4oz(110g) sultanas
4oz(110g) currants
4oz(110g) seedless raisins
2oz(50g) chopped mixed peel
(or use 14oz(450g) of dried Mixed
Fruit in place of the ingredients above.)
2oz(50g) chopped glace cherries

2oz(50g) ground almonds
9oz(250g) plain flour
8oz(225g) butter at room temperature
1 tspn baking powder
8oz(225g) caster sugar
3 standard eggs beaten
1 tblspn sherry, brandy or milk

For the top of the cake, 1oz(25g) blanched and halved almonds. Grease and line a 7 inch (18mm) cake tin with greaseproof paper.

Mix all the dried fruits with the ground almonds and pour over the sherry or brandy.

Cream the butter and sugar and gradually add in the beaten eggs. Sift the flour and baking powder and stir it into the creamed mixture. Add the dried

DUNDEE CAKE *cont.*

fruit. Combine the mixture thoroughly and put it into the baking tin. Slightly hollow the centre (which will rise) and cover the top with a pattern of almond halves.

Bake for $2^{1}/_{2}$ to 3 hours at 325F/160C/Gas Mark 3. Test with a skewer which should come out clean. If not cooked, return to a slightly cooler oven for a further 30 minutes. An uncooked cake will be "sizzling" if you hold your ear to the centre! Cool the cake in the tin and then turn it onto a wire rack. Cool it thoroughly before storing.

ORFAR FRUIT LOAF

4oz(110g) butter
4oz(110g) caster sugar
1 standard egg, beaten
8oz(225g) plain flour
1 tspn baking powder
1 tblspn milk
4oz(110g) sultanas
4oz(110g) currants
1oz(25g) chopped almonds

Grease and line a 1lb(450g) loaf tin.

Cream the butter and sugar. Add beaten egg in small amounts as spoonfuls of the flour is combined with the mixture. Only add the baking powder with the last amount of flour. Stir in the milk and then the fruit and almonds and combine thoroughly. Put into the baking tin and depress the centre just slightly.

Bake for $1^1/_2$–2 hours, or until a skewer comes out cleanly, 350F/180C/ Gas Mark between 4–5. Cool on a wire rack.

This is best eaten as cooked, on the same day, resembling a tea loaf rather than a rich cake.

SHETLAND BRIDE'S BONN OR BRIDAL CAKE

5oz(150g) self raising flour
1oz(25g) caster sugar
2oz(50g) butter
$^1/_2$ tspn caraway seeds
milk

Rub the butter into the sifted flour. Add the sugar and caraway seeds. Use enough milk to make a soft pliable dough. Turn out onto a well floured board and keep your hands well floured as you lightly form a round of about $^3/_4$ inch thick. Score deeply into four quarters or farls.

Bake on a hot girdle for about five minutes each side. Cool on a cloth on a wire rack. It should be eaten the same day.

This bun was traditionally broken over the bride's head as she entered her new home, the pieces being eaten by her and her new husband.

CLOUTIE DUMPLING

This is probably the most famous of all the Scots recipes –
it sounds romantic and rustic! The trouble is there are so many
variations of this traditional dish. Each household might claim its own
species, born of generations of trial and experience. As with most recipes
using dried fruit and spices, it was the special treat for Hogmanay,
especially in the Highlands and Islands though today it can be
bought in slices from village butchers.

The "clout" is the cloth in which the pudding is wrapped
for boiling. When the dumpling really was cooked in the pot over the
fire it was "dried off" on a plate in front of the fire after cooking.
Then, when life was so simple that the one fire in the "hoose"
provided for both heat and cooking, the amount of time required to cook a
Cloutie Dumpling was neither here nor there. Later,
I include a more modern approach.

Here are some traditional variations –
use them as a base to make your own.

$\mathcal{T}$RADITIONAL CLOUTIE DUMPLING

3oz(75g) flour	*2oz(50g) currants*
3oz(75g) breadcrumbs	*2oz(50g) brown sugar*
3oz(75g) chopped suet	*1 tblspn syrup*
1 tspn ground cinnamon	*$^1/_2$ tspn bicarbonate of soda*
$^1/_2$ tspn ground ginger	*about 6oz(170ml) freshly*
(or nutmeg if preferred)	*soured milk or buttermilk*
2oz(50g) sultanas	

Mix all the ingredients to make a fairly soft batter. Dip a large piece of cotton cloth into boiling water; wring it and dredge with flour. Set the cloth into a basin and spoon in the batter. Draw up the cloth evenly, leaving a space to allow the pudding to swell, and tie tightly with string.

Put a plate into the bottom of the steaming pan and put the dumpling onto this. Pour boiling water up to $^3/_4$ the way up the dumpling and simmer for 2–$2^1/_2$ hours, adding more boiling water as required.

To serve the dumpling: remove from boiling water and dip into cold water for a second to prevent the dumpling sticking to the cloth. Put the dumpling into a bowl and remove the string and open out the cloth. Put a warmed plate over the top and invert. Remove the cloth carefully and if necessary, dry off the dumpling in the oven. Dredge with caster sugar and serve with hot custard.

CLOUTIE DUMPLING WITHOUT SUET

6oz(175g) butter or margarine
12oz(350g) flour
6oz(175g) sugar
1 tspn baking powder
1 tspn cinnamon
1 tspn ground ginger

1lb(450g) sultanas
8oz(225g) currants
1 tblspn treacle
1 tblspn syrup
2 eggs beaten
milk to mix

Mix the dry ingredients and rub in the batter. Add the fruits and stir thoroughly. Into a well in the centre add the beaten eggs and the syrup mixing into a stiff consistency with only a little milk.

Proceed as above to boil the pudding. This quantity will take a good 3 hours.

Cloutie dumplings can be cooked in greased pudding bowls in the same way as traditional steamed puddings.

Left-over dumpling is sliced and fried with bacon and eggs for breakfast – hence its appearance in butcher's shops!

*C*LOUTIE DUMPLING WITH NAE CLOUT!

Into a saucepan put:

12oz(350g) mixed fruit	*1 tspn bicarbonate of soda*
4oz(110g) sugar	*1 tspn mixed spice*
8floz(220ml) water	*$^1/_2$ tspn cinnamon*
4oz(110g) butter or margarine	*$^1/_2$ tspn nutmeg*

Bring this to the boil and simmer steadily for 12 minutes. Cool the mixture to warm.

Add: *2 eggs beaten, mixing well, and alternatively, spoonful by spoonful*
    4oz(110g) plain flour and
    4oz(110g) self raising flour
    Mix well.

Pour into a greased and paper lined round tin. Drop the tin onto the bench to settle the fruit. Bake at 325F/170C/Gas Mark 3 for 1–1$^1/_2$ hours. A skewer should come out cleanly and the fruit should have stopped sizzling. You may need to rest the cake for a further 15 minutes after turning off the heat and leaving the oven door ajar.

The recipe was given to me by a neighbour in Australia and I have since come across the same recipe with minor alterations time and time again.

0TH CENTURY CLOUTIE DUMPLING

For the Microwave:

2oz(50g) margarine	*(sultanas, currants, raisins)*
4oz(110g) self raising flour	*2 large tspns syrup*
2oz(50g) sugar	*(which will be close to a tablespoon)*
¹/₂ tspn cinnamon	*1 egg beaten*
¹/₂ tspn nutmeg	*milk if required*
8oz(225g) dried fruits	

U se an electric blender to 'rub' in the margarine with the flour and sugar and spices. Tip into a large bowl and mix in the dried fruits. Into a well in the centre add the syrup and the beaten egg. Work in with wooden spoon, picking up all the dry ingredients. The mixture should be quite wet. If not add 2 tspns of milk.

Lightly grease a 2 pint microwave pudding bowl; a plastic one is best. Fill the bowl to about, or just over ³/₄ full. Cover with Microwave Clear Wrap very loosely, pull it up to a peak to allow the pudding to expand.

Put the dumpling into a microwave at Mark 8 for about 5 minutes, turning after half time if the machine does not have a turntable. Take off the plastic, rest for a minute or so, and then cook for a further 1 to 2 minutes on High. The top should appear dry and the sides should have just 'pulled away'. (Times are for a 700Watt microwave – adjust times to suit your machine.)

Now comes the advantage of a plastic dish. The dumpling is still cooking! Roll the pudding dish so that air circulates round the sides of the dumpling. Jolt it lightly so that air gets under the bottom of the dumpling. Allowing air to get to the dumpling will halt the cooking process earlier and allow the dumpling to come loose easily. It also provides a close approximation of the 'skin' which forms over the traditional pudding. Turn the dumpling on to a wire rack.

It is important to note the microwaved dumpling will 'crumble' more readily than its slowly steamed counterpart. But the modern Scots housewife is also likely to be crumbling round the edges – holding down a job and ancient Scots traditions both at the same time is nobody's idea of fun. If Cloutie Dumpling appears at Hogmanay in your house, guests will be so impressed, none should be left for breakfast next morning! If the whisky was good, no-one will want breakfast!

The microwaved cloutie which follows was supplied by a friend who uses her mother's traditional recipe. The ingredients are extremely simple and no syrups are used. It has a dense very moist texture.

MAGGIE'S MICROWAVED CLOUTIE

1lb(450g) self raising flour
6oz(175) sugar
pinch of salt
2 tspns mixed spice
6oz(175g) suet – or vegetarian suet
1lb(450g) dried fruit – currants and raisins
approximately 20floz(600ml) water to mix

Mix all the ingredients. Sprinkle the centre of a wet cloth with flour and place the mixture in the centre. Tie the cloth and place the pudding in a large microwavable bowl. Cover with boiling water.

Cook for about 5 minutes at high and reduce to medium. Cook for approximately 25 minutes.

You can test the pudding from its firmness and times will have to be adjusted to suit the individual microwave.

This makes a large cloutie. You may like to halve the ingredients. Cook for 3 minutes on high and reduce to medium, cooking for a further 15–20 minutes.

 WEET HAGGIS

8oz(225g) medium oatmeal
4oz(110g) flour
8oz(225g) chopped suet
2oz(50g) brown sugar
2oz(50g) currants
2oz(50g) raisins
salt and pepper
water to mix

Bind all the dry ingredients with sufficient water to make a stiff mixture. Place in a greased 2 pint(1 litre) pudding bowl and cover with a round of greaseproof paper and aluminium foil. Secure tightly with string. Put the bowl into a pan of boiling water so that the water reaches $^3/_4$ the way up the bowl. Cover and simmer for about 3 hours. Serve hot.

As with left-over Cloutie Dumpling, this dish from Ayrshire is traditionally used up at breakfast time, sliced and fried, or warmed in the oven.

PUDDINGS, DESSERTS AND SWEET TREATS

Visit any of the kitchens in a Scottish castle or
stately home and you will see the vast array of pie dishes,
pudding bowls and brass moulds.

When I read an old recipe I am reminded of the
tremendous effort that was required to bake these desserts.
Imagine the huge solid cone of sugar … 'of pounded and
sifted loaf sugar, take one pound …'. Imagine life without
an electric mixer … 'beat all well together
for twenty to thirty minutes …'.

Traditions in desserts as we know them today really
began in the eighteenth and nineteenth century though there
is an age old heritage of simple seasonal treats.

APPLE FRUSHIE

Frushie means crumbly and refers to the texture of the pastry. Other fruits may be used in season.

Pastry: *8oz(225g) plain flour*
2oz(50g) butter
2oz(50g) lard
pinch of salt
cold water

Sift the flour and salt and rub in the butter and lard. Use sufficient cold water to make a soft dough. Chill for 30 minutes.

Use $^3/_4$ of the dough to line a flan ring or shallow dish. Use the remaining dough to cut long strips which will be used for the latticed top.

Filling: *12oz(375 thinly sliced cooking apples* *2 tblspns clear honey* *1 tblspn rose-water*	*Arrange the thin apple slices over the pastry base.* *Sprinkle the honey and rose-water over the fruit.*

Lay the pastry strips across the top in a latticed pattern and bake in an oven at 400F/200C/Gas Mark 6, for 30 minutes.

Sprinkle with caster sugar and serve with cream.

MORAYSHIRE APPLES

This closely resembles a 'crumble' and you may wish to substitute butter for the suet.

The Filling: *1 1/2 lb(675g) cooking apples*

5floz(150ml) water

4oz(100g) caster sugar

pinch of ground cloves

Gently dissolve the sugar in the water with the ground cloves in a saucepan over a low heat.

Peel core and slice the apples and arrange in a large pie dish.

Pour the sugar syrup over the apples.

The Topping: *6oz(175g) medium oatmeal*

3oz(75g) shredded suet, or butter if preferred

2oz(50g) soft brown sugar

2oz(50g) chopped hazelnuts

Mix all the ingredients, (rub in the butter if used instead of suet) and spread over the apples. Press down gently and sprinkle a little more brown sugar over the top.

Bake in an oven at 350F/180C/Gas Mark 4 for about an hour.

Serve hot with cream.

MARMALADE TART

Pastry: *6oz(175g) plain flour*
3oz(75g) butter
1 tblspn caster sugar (optional)
cold water to mix

Rub the butter into the flour until the mixture resembles fine breadcrumbs. Mix in the caster sugar if used. Use a knife and add a little water to bind the dough. Knead for a few seconds to make the dough smooth. Roll out and line a flan ring.

Filling: *3 eggs beaten*
4 tblspns milk
4 tblspns Dundee marmalade,
or other dark marmalade
2oz(50g) butter, melted
2oz(50g) caster sugar

Combine all the above ingredients thoroughly and pour into the pastry case. Bake at 400F/200C/Gas Mark 6 for 10 minutes and for a further 30 minutes at the reduced temperature, 325F/160C/Gas Mark 3.

HOLYROOD PUDDING

20floz(600ml) milk
2oz(50g) semolina
1oz(50g) butter
3oz(75g) caster sugar
2oz(50g) ratafia biscuits
2 tblspns orange marmalade
3 eggs, separated

Bring the milk to boiling point in a large saucepan. Stir in the semolina, the sugar and the butter. Allow to simmer gently for about five minutes, stirring constantly. Leave to cool.

Beat the egg whites until stiff.

Into the slightly cooled mixture add the egg yolks and the marmalade and mix thoroughly. Mix in the ratafia biscuits and lastly, using a metal spoon, fold in the egg whites.

Pour the mixture into a large buttered pie dish and bake for 20 to 30 minutes at 350F/180C/Gas Mark 4. The pudding should be set and golden brown on top.

$\mathcal{C}$ALEDONIAN CREAM

10floz(300ml) double, or
whipping cream
2 tblspns brandy or malt whisky
2 tblspns orange marmalade
1 tblspn lemon juice
1oz(25g) caster sugar

Combine the brandy, marmalade, lemon juice and sugar and add the cream last. Whip the mixture until it is thick.

Spoon into glasses and chill before serving.

$\mathcal{E}$DINBURGH FOG

10floz(300ml) double, or
whipping cream
1oz(25g) ratafia biscuits
1oz(25g) blanched chopped
almonds
1oz(25g) caster sugar
a few drops pure vanilla essence
almond slivers for decoration

Beat the cream with the sugar and vanilla essence until it is stiff. Mix in the ratafias and the almonds. Decorate with almond slivers.

Spoon into glasses and serve chilled.

CRANACHAN

3–4oz(75–100g) slightly toasted and sifted oatmeal
10floz(300ml) double or whipping cream
1 tblspn malt whisky (or rum if preferred)
6oz(175g) raspberries or blackberries

Whip the cream. Pour the whisky over the oatmeal and fold the mixture into the cream. Fold in the fruit reserving a few pieces for decoration.

Serve in glasses, chilled.

Here the simplest ingredients are used with the traditional staple of oats to make a festive treat.

Cranachan or Cream-Crowdie was eaten at harvest time, the time of plenty. At Hallowe'en small charms were stirred into the cranachan bringing the finders good luck.

The following recipe is more elaborate
and makes an elegant dessert.

CREAM-CROWDIE OR CRANACHAN

2oz(50g) lightly toasted and sifted oatmeal
4 tblspns malt whisky
2 tblspns thick heather honey
2oz(50g) crowdie, or cream cheese
5floz(150ml) double cream
6–8oz(175–200g) raspberries or other soft fruit
clear heather honey for decoration

Mix the oatmeal, whisky and thick honey together and leave in a covered bowl overnight.

Mix in the crowdie or soft cream cheese. Fold in the raspberries.

Whip the cream until it is stiff.

To serve:

Place a spoonful of cream in the bottom of individual wine glasses. Add a portion of the crowdie mixture and cover with more cream. Over the top drizzle a little clear honey. Chill before serving.

SCOTCH TRIFLE

6 trifle sponges
raspberry jam
3–4oz(75–100g) crumbled
ratafia biscuits
grated rind of $^1/_2$ a lemon
3floz(90ml) sweet sherry
2floz(60ml) brandy

20floz(600ml) rich custard, cold
5floz(150ml) double cream
1 tspn caster sugar
1 tspn Drambuie, or a few drops
of vanilla essence
cherries, angelica, chopped nuts
or choice of decoration

Split the trifle sponges and spread generously with raspberry jam. Sandwich the sponges together again and arrange them in the bottom of a trifle dish. Sprinkle the crumbled ratafias and the grated lemon rind over the sponges. Combine the sherry and brandy and pour this over the sponges. Leave to soak for at least an hour.

Beat the cold custard to a creamy consistency and spread it evenly over the sponges.

Whip the cream with the sugar and Drambuie (or vanilla essence) until it is firm.

Spread it over the custard.

Decorate and serve chilled.

 BURNT CREAM

20floz(600ml) double cream
yolks of 4 large eggs
3 tblspns caster sugar
vanilla essence
caster sugar for topping

Beat the egg yolks and sugar together and add a drop or two of vanilla essence.

Bring the cream to just about boiling and slowly add it to the beaten egg mixture, beating steadily at the same time.

Pour the mixture into a shallow ovenproof dish and set this in a roasting pan with hot water reaching about halfway up the sides of the pudding dish. Cover the top with greaseproof paper and cook for about 40 minutes at 350F/180C/Gas Mark 4 or until it is slightly set. Cool overnight.

Sprinkle the top of the cream with a thick layer of caster sugar and place the dish under a preheated grill so that the sugar melts and becomes caramelized. Leave once again to cool so that the 'burnt' sugar becomes hard.

This dessert has long been associated with Trinity College, Cambridge. In fact it originated from a country house in the Aberdeenshire district in the mid nineteenth century.

URNEY PUDDING

4oz(100g) plain flour
4oz(100g) butter
2oz(50g) caster sugar
1 tspn bicarbonate of soda
1 tblspn milk
2 tblspns strawberry jam
2 eggs, beaten

Sift the flour. Cream the butter and sugar. Add the flour gradually and the eggs, beating all the time. Mix in the jam.

Dissolve the bicarbonate of soda in the milk and add to the mixture. Beat thoroughly.

Put the mixture into a greased pudding bowl, (it should not be much over half full), and cover with greased paper. Steam for $1\frac{1}{2}$ hours.

Serve with custard.

SWEETIES

Berwick Cockles, Boilings, Curly Murlies, Glessie, Hawick Balls, Jeddart Snails, Oddfellows, Soor Plums, are all "sweeties" and just a few of the many varieties in the traditional confectionery of Scotland.

While some sweets were made by bakers and confectioners and were regional specialities most sweets were made at home. Enterprising women who made up the treats to sell were affectionately known as "Sweetie-Wives".

EDINBURGH ROCK

1lb(450g) granulated sugar
$^1/_2$ tspn cream of tartar
7floz(200ml) water

Flavours and colours; peppermint,
raspberry, ginger, lemon etc.
Icing sugar

Over a low heat dissolve the sugar in the water. Add the cream of tartar.

Boil until the temperature reaches 260F/130C. The mixture will form a hard ball when dropped into cold water.

Remove from the heat and add chosen flavour and colour. Cool a little.

Pour onto an oiled surface, traditionally a marble slab.

Using an oiled knife or scraper turn the edges of the mixture into the centre, continuing this folding over until the mixture is cool enough to handle.

Dust the mixture with icing sugar and using your hands pull up and let it drop back. Repeat until the mixture becomes opaque and hardens.

Finally pull into one long piece about $^1/_2$ inch(1cm) thick and cut into shorter lengths.

Place on a tray sprinkled with icing sugar and dust the rock with more icing sugar.

The rock should be left in a warm atmosphere for up to a week when it will crumble when bitten.

Store in an airtight tin or jar.

GLASGOW TOFFEE

4oz(100g) butter
8oz(225g) sugar
5floz(150ml) milk
6oz(175g) golden syrup
2oz(50g) dark chocolate
¹/₂ tspn vanilla essence

Using a large saucepan, melt the butter over a low heat. Add the sugar, milk, syrup and pieces of chocolate stirring until the sugar has dissolved.

Increase the heat and bring the mixture to the boil, stirring continually until the temperature reaches 250F/120C. The mixture will form a hard ball when dropped into cold water.

Remove from the heat and allow the mixture to cool before stirring in the vanilla essence.

Pour into a greased shallow tray and allow to almost set. Cut into squares.

Once the toffee has become hard, wrap in waxed paper and store in an airtight container.

UTTERSCOTCH

1lb(450g) Demerara sugar
4oz(100g) butter
5floz(150ml) water
juice of $^1/_2$ a lemon

Put all the ingredients into a large saucepan and, over a low heat, stir until the butter has melted and the sugar dissolved.

Bring to the boil and simmer, stirring continually for between 15 and 20 minutes. Test the mixture by dropping a little into a cup of cold water. It should harden.

Remove from the heat and beat for a few minutes to assist the cooling process.

Pour into a greased tray and allow to cool. Mark into squares before it is entirely set.

When set and cold, break into squares and store in an airtight container.

HELENSBURGH TOFFEE

4oz(125g) butter
5floz(150ml) water
2lb(1kg) granulated sugar
1 tblspn golden syrup
7$^1/_2$ floz(200ml) condensed milk
vanilla essence
walnut halves for decoration (optional)

In a large saucepan, over a low heat, melt the butter in the water and stir in the syrup and sugar. Heat gently and stir continually until the sugar has dissolved. Do not allow to boil.

Stir in the condensed milk and gradually bring to simmering point. Continue stirring until the temperature reaches 240F/120C. Test a drop of the mixture which will form a soft ball in a cup of cold water.

Remove from the heat and cool slightly before adding the vanilla essence. Beat the mixture until it becomes thicker, the colour becomes pale and the texture slightly grainy.

Pour into a greased tray. Cool a little and decorate with walnut halves if liked. Cut into squares when thoroughly cold and set.

This is a rich confection rather more like a fudge than a toffee.

ABLET

4oz(125g) butter
1lb(450g) granulated sugar
10floz(300ml) milk
vanilla essence

In a large saucepan gently dissolve the sugar in the milk. Then bring to the boil and simmer for about 20 minutes, stirring constantly. Test by dropping a small drop of the mixture into a cup of cold water. A soft ball should form.

Remove from the heat and add the butter and the vanilla essence. Beat the mixture until it becomes thicker, paler and more grainy.

Pour into a greased tray and allow to set.

Cut into squares and store in an airtight container.

WISS MILK TABLET

1lb(450g) sugar
2oz(50g) butter
4floz(125ml) milk
$7^{1}/_{2}$ f loz(200ml) condensed milk
vanilla essence

In a large saucepan gently melt the butter in the milk. Add the sugar and stir until dissolved. Bring to the boil and allow to boil for 10 minutes.

Stir in the condensed milk and boil for a further 10 minutes. Remove from the heat.

Beat steadily for a few minutes adding the vanilla essence. The mixture will start to thicken. Pour into a greased tray and mark it into squares.

Allow to set and cut the squares. Store in an airtight container.

LAVOURED TABLET

4oz(100g) butter
10floz(300ml) milk
2lb(1kg) caster sugar
7$^{1}/_{2}$ floz(200ml) condensed milk
Flavour of choice: oil of cinnamon,
peppermint, ginger, lemon, nuts

In a large saucepan melt the butter in the water over a low heat. Add the sugar and gently bring to the boil stirring constantly.

Add the condensed milk and simmer gently, stirring constantly, for about 20 minutes. Test a small drop of the mixture in a cup of cold water. A soft ball should form.

Remove from the heat, add your choice of flavour and beat steadily until the mixture becomes thick.

Pour into a greased tray and mark into squares. When cold, cut the squares and store in an airtight container.

INDEX

 OTES FOR AMERICAN COOKS

The American Pint is 16 fluid oz.,while the British Pint is 20 fluid oz.
The American Tablespoon holds 14.2 ml compared to the British 17.7 ml.
The teaspoon measure is the same in both countries.

A General Guide

Plain flour is known as All -purpose flour and Self- Raising Flour
is known as All pupose self -raising flour.

8oz flour = $2\frac{1}{2}$ cups.

8oz oatmeal, fine or medium = 2 cup

8oz sugar, granulated, caster, = $1\frac{1}{4}$ cups

8oz soft brown (light brown)sugar= $1\frac{1}{4}$ cups

8oz butter = 1 cup

8oz suet = 2 cups.

20fl oz = $2\frac{1}{2}$ cups

8oz dried fruits = $1\frac{1}{2}$ cups

2oz dried almonds, flaked, ground = $\frac{1}{2}$ cup

6oz golden syrup (light corn syrup)= $\frac{1}{2}$ cup

8oz treacle (molasses)= $\frac{3}{4}$ cup

NOTES